Lessons Learned from Girdles on How to Do Friendships

TOWERA LOPER

Girdle Girlfriends
Lessons Learned from Girdles on How to Do Friendships

Copyright © 2016 Towera Loper
All rights reserved.

Published by:
NyreePress Literary Group
Fort Worth, TX 76161
1-800-972-3864
www.nyreepress.com

All rights reserved. No part of this book may be used or reproduced by any means, graphic, electronic, or mechanical, including photocopying, recording, taping or by any information storage retrieval system without the written permission of the publisher. Copying this book is both illegal and unethical.

ISBN 13: 978-1-945304-18-7
ISBN-10: 1-945304-18-9
Library of Congress Control Number: pending

Christian Living / Inspirational

Printed in the United States of America

Contents

Foreword by Janeen L. McBath 5
Acknowledgments 7
Introduction 9

Part 1: The Research

Chapter 1   The Sisterhood of Girdles and Girlfriends 13
Chapter 2   How to Shop for Girdles and Girlfriends 19

Part 2: Shopper's Guide

Chapter 3   The Right Style 23
Chapter 4   Try It on First 33
Chapter 5   Fit Matters 39

Part 3: Benefits of Girdles

Chapter 6   Improves Your Posture 47
Chapter 7   You Move Freely 55
Chapter 8   The Muffin Top Concealer 63

Part 4: Girdle Care

Chapter 9   Wash on Gentle 71
Chapter 10   Rotation Plan 79
Chapter 11   The Right Detergent 85

Part 5: Final Thought

Chapter 12   What Kind of Girdle Are You? 91

NOTES 95

Foreword by Janeen L. McBath

I met Towera more than fifteen years ago while she was attending Regent University in Virginia Beach. I watched how Towera connected her passion for reaching out to others within our local church. I am delighted that Towera chose to share her knowledge and experience of the importance of true friendships through Girdle Girlfriends. Her vulnerability and profound insight will encourage women to take a R.I.S.K. while building a community of caring friends. In doing so, they are taking the Responsibility of stepping out of their comfort zone, taking the Initiative in showing someone they may not know personally how to receive love, being willing to make the Sacrifice to give freely in order to establish a healthy relationship, and gaining the Knowledge to understand that a true love exchange happens when we open ourselves up to others, even when we may feel it puts us in a vulnerable state.

Towera will draw back the curtain and give a glimpse into the heart of this subject as she allows the reader to journey with her through her own personal friendships. It is evident that in reading this book, you will be challenged to take the risk of developing healthy relationships and a renewed mind, and that your spirit will be lifted by a life-altering encounter with the God of Girdle Girlfriends. Many other individuals may have similar experiences on their journey, but the courageous inspiration in Towera's message is rare.

Towera's genuine passion is that your views of friendships will be fortified by God's amazing love and your willingness to allow others into your world. Be blessed as you turn each page and allow new insight to be revealed on this journey as we see more clearly. "Friends come and friends go, but a true friend sticks by you like family" (Proverbs 18:24, MSG).

Acknowledgments

I am honored to have written this book because, by writing it, it made me realize that it's not about what people say about what you can and cannot do, but it's realizing that when God plants a vision of writing in your heart, the only person who can stop you is you. This book is a reflection of my willingness to believe that small voice from God saying, "You can do this!" So I thank God, who deserves all the credit, for giving me the ability to pen these chapters down.

Additional gratitude and thanks go out to the following people:

- Calvin, my husband and best friend, for being my greatest cheerleader in this process. Your gentle nudging and utmost faith in me through this process have made it all possible. I love you.

- Pastor Janeen McBath, the inspiration behind this book. Through your sharing, this seed was birthed, and I am forever grateful to you for being the catalyst.

- Beatrice B. Nyirenda, my mother, whom I love with every fiber of my being. Thank you for raising me to be the woman I am today. You are priceless. I love you.

- Tiwonge Nyirenda and Tafika Haambote, my young sisters, for demonstrating this kind of friendship. I love you, and I am glad that I get to be a part of your lives.

- ALL the ladies who shared their stories with me. This book would not be possible if you were not willing to share your hearts with me. Thank you.

- To Kara Franco, my copyeditor. Thank you for taking on this project. Your meticulous attention to detail is a work of art. Forever grateful.

- Kennisha Hill, NyreePress Literary Group, my publisher and her entire staff for making it possible for women to be holding this book in their hands. Thank you for accepting me into the Nyree family.

- Last but not least, to my girdle girlfriends. You cried with me when life was hard, you encouraged me when I was walking in doubt, you stood by me when it seemed as though the world was crushing in on me, you listened to me when I was just rambling on! To you, I owe my life. I love you.

Introduction

It was a Wednesday afternoon, and a few ladies came together over lunch to hear my Pastor, Janeen McBath, talk about the importance of females having meaningful relationships. It was the second time I was listening to this discussion because the inner workings of relationships fascinate me on all levels. As a student, I was eager to learn a thing or two about becoming better at relationships. As she shared her thoughts, she made this reference: **"You need to have a girl-friend who is like a girdle-TIGHT! She holds you together and does not allow things to 'fall out.' She is there to protect you and does not expose your issues."**

I remember all of us chuckling and clapping after she made that statement as she graciously carried on. However, for some odd reason, I found myself parked on that statement. My mind wandered off as I thought about the implications. In that moment, I knew that something had changed. I had to write something about girdle girlfriends. I did not know what, but I committed it to prayer and believed that I would get direction moving onwards on how to unpack the richness of that metaphor.

The need for these connections cannot be ignored, overlooked or underestimated, because the fabric that runs through the human DNA is relationships. We were created to be relational beings. We were made for companionship. We see the first glimpse of this need and reality stemming from the creator of the universe in Genesis 2:18 when He says to Himself, "*It is not good for man to be alone, I'll make him a helper, a companion.*" (MSG). Granted, this text is mostly used in the context of a husband and wife relationship, but the principle of companionship is obvious.

Suffice it to say, one cannot compare the human need for relationship to that of a girdle, or assume that every woman owns, let alone wears one. However, one can be amazed by the simple truths they can learn after one considers the functioning of a girdle—one being that it enhances and accentuates your body.

A few things come to mind when I think about girdles: the Oscars, the Emmys, and the Tony Awards, to mention but a few. Some of the Hollywood actresses have admitted after the show that they had to wear a girdle to fit into their outfit. The purpose of the girdle in that moment is to make sure that the body is shaped evenly to fit into that stunning dress by Vera Wang, Versace, Oscar de la Renta, etc.

The naked eye does not see the girdles, but we are given the opportunity to observe their appearances throughout the show. The ladies elegantly walk the red carpet, waving to the crowd, looking stunning and elegant as the girdle fits perfectly in shape with their body. Now imagine yourself on the red carpet of life surrounded by friends who fit you like that girdle, holding you together, and allowing you to blossom; a friendship that adds such great qualities; assets like love, trust, hope, and confidence.

Yes, it's work to get ready for the Oscars because all eyes are on them. I have heard that sometimes it takes all day to get ready for an event that will last only three to four hours, tops. But to them, it's worth every minute of it to have that one experience. Such is the case with developing meaningful relationships. It takes time, commitment, and energy to make it work. But, when all is said and done, it will be worth it.

Chapter 1
The Sisterhood of Girdles and Girlfriends

"A friendship can weather most things and thrive in thin soil; but it needs a little mulch of letters and phone calls and small, silly presents every so often - just to save it from drying out completely."

Pam Brown

I came across a very interesting article from the Mayo Clinic; it was on friendship and titled, "Friendships: Enrich Your Life and Improve Your Health." For those not familiar with the Mayo Clinic, it is based in Minnesota and is widely regarded as one of the world's greatest hospitals and ranked number one on the U.S. News & World Report List of "Best Hospitals." The research asserts that one of the benefits of friendships is health and well-being: "Friendships can have a major impact on your health and well-being, but it's not always easy to build or maintain friendships. Understand the importance of friendships in your life and what you can do to develop and nurture friendships."

As I write this book, I have a dear friend who is battling an illness. As she walks through this difficult season of her life, I have seen how her friends have rallied around her, taking turns to spend the night with her at the hospital while her husband takes care of their eleven-year-old twins. Every morning for the past two weeks, I have been waking up to the text messages that she has been sending to her close-knit friends.

She always starts with a greeting: "Good Morning Team Bradshaw," and she proceeds to tell us how she is feeling that day. We each take turns to respond and encourage her on this fight. I know, beyond a shadow of a doubt, that our friendship and support towards her and her family has a positive impact on her life because she has a support system. She has companionship. She can trust and depend on us to help her each minute, even when it gets rough sometimes.

I just got a text from her the other day stating, "I need my friends! It is filling in the empty places. I will keep praying and trusting God…Thank you sooooo much. I really needed to hear from you today." Friendship! Meaningful relationships! Our dear sister has found a place of rest among her friends. The Mayo Clinic is definitely onto something when it says that friendships enrich your life and improve your health.

Deborah is another person who has found improved health for her chronic illness through social media. She shares her struggle by giving us a glimpse into her life by stating that she used to lie awake at night with "agonizing, shooting nerve pain," feeling helpless and alone. She began going online, where she found others who were also awake and in pain; they became her "midnight friends."

Through this process, she became a part of a large and growing group of people with chronic illness in the U.S. who are using the Internet and other online technology to take charge of, and improve, their own health. How is this possible? Because you know that you are not alone in this fight, and that realization gives you the strength to fight on for a healthier you.

I love the perspective Leslie Parrott gives on friendship and women. "The truth is, as women, we are uniquely designed by God to lean into soul friendships. This isn't just a spiritual and emotional difference, but one that is woven into the very chemistry of our body [...] in short, we have a God-given need for soul friendships that is more ancient than the Celtic world. And because of it, we can trust that there is great purpose and fulfillment in the give-and-take of these deep-spirited relationships." Below are some health benefits of friendship from the Mayo Clinic article:

Benefits of Having Friendships

- Increase your sense of belonging and purpose.

- Boost your happiness and reduce your stress.

- Improve your self-confidence and self-worth.

- Help you cope with traumas, like divorce, serious illness, job loss, or a loved one's death.

- Encourage you to change or avoid unhealthy lifestyle habits, such as excessive drinking or lack of exercise.

Having addressed some benefits of friendships as it pertains to health, how then, do girdles serve as a health agent for our bodies? On healthable.org, under the title "The Emotional and Physical Health Benefits of Wearing a Girdle," it gives us a few insights into how this is possible.

Health Benefits to Wearing Girdles

- **A Supportive Hug:** "The deep pressure provided by the girdle is similar to the therapy sometimes provided by occupational therapists."

- **A Source of Back Support**: Girdles can reduce "headaches, migraines, tension in neck and shoulders."

- **Abdominal Support:** "Sometimes girdles are recommended to men and women who are recovering from surgery because of these supportive qualities."

- **An Effective Weight-Loss Aid:** "The girdle can help you to control your appetite, reduce your serving size, and serve as a general reminder of weight loss goals."

- **Confidence Boosting:** "You can't deny that when you feel good about yourself, everything else seems to fall into place. If you think that you look good, you are more likely to tackle harder tasks, get the raise you deserve, or approach another person confidently."

What amazes me as I see the comparisons between girdles and friendships, is what they do, not only for your health but also for your soul. Is it not refreshing to see what friendships bring to the table? The sad truth is that some women do not think they need friendships because of what they have gone through in life. They have been hurt in past relationships. They cut off relationships and chose not to engage with their hearts because they viewed themselves as victims.

Andy Stanley says it best: "It's these feelings of victimization that fuel our justifications and excuses. A victim will always have an excuse [...] And so pain and hurt create an unassailable wall of excuses and rationalizations." I am in no way minimizing what brought you to this point, but staying there is not healthy either.

I would like to suggest that the "refusal" to have friends sucks the life out of you because you were created for relationships, and your refusal to have meaningful relationships deprives you of an abundant life. Be brave and willing to make friends. This brings us to our next chapter, "How to Shop for Girdles and Friendships."

The Shopper's Guide

A shopper's guide is meant to assist the public on how to better decide which items are best for the consumer. For the most part, it does the homework for you, so you spend less time doing the research, and you focus on narrowing down what best speaks to the product you want or need to get. The same is true for girdles and friendships. We have given ideas on how to shop for both, and the following chapters will unpack a few of these findings.

Chapter 2
How to Shop for Girdles and Girlfriends

"I've never been socially outgoing, but I suspect I've gotten more and more ambivalent about making new friends. I'm irritated by how-do-you-do chit-chat, but that's how new relationships usually begin."

Ariel Gore

It can be difficult to find the type of shapewear one needs. You have to be willing to go to different stores to find what will compliment your figure. Inconvenient? No doubt. Worth the search? Absolutely! Thankfully, there are so many places you can shop for girdles because there is a demand for them. Department stores from Target to Dillard's carry shapewear.

What is fascinating is that there are different types of shapewear (e.g., for post-partum, post-surgical, butt lifters, and posture correctors just to mention but a few). What is critical to shopping for one is to know exactly why you need that particular shapewear. Your success in shopping for a girdle is contingent on what your body needs. The website eHow.com guides us on how to shop for girdles. For a complete listing, please visit the website.

How to Buy a Girdle

- Measure your body to get correct hip, thigh and waist sizes.
- Decide if you need a thigh, hip, or a buttock girdle.
- Determine the size girdle needed for your personal reasons.
- Visit an undergarment store that specializes in properly fitting people for bras and girdles.
- Purchase at least two or three girdles when you make your selections.

Now that we have been given a guide on how to shop for shapewear, let us consider how we shop for friends as suggested by the Mayo Clinic. A detailed list can be found on its website.

Ways to Meet People

- Attend community events. Find a group with similar interests in an activity, such as auto racing, gardening, reading or making crafts.
- Volunteer. You can form strong connections when you work with people who have mutual interests.
- Extend and accept invitations. Contact someone who recently invited you to an activity and return the favor.
- Take up a new interest. Take a college or community education course to meet people who have similar interests.
- Join a faith community. Take advantage of special activities and get-to-know-you events for new members.
- Take a walk. Grab your kids or pet and head outside. Chat with neighbors who are also out and about, or head to a popular park and strike up conversations there.

About ninety percent of my closest friendships were formed in an academic or faith-based community. I remember sitting next to Sara at our new student orientation. I never knew her from Adam. I remember just having small talk about nothing meaningful. A few days later when I went to start my part-time job at the university, I found Sara working in the same department!

Gradually, our friendship developed over the next few months due to being in the same classes and working the same hours. Needless to say, sixteen years later, I call her my sister from another mother. Our skin tones and ethnicity are night and day, but what I can say is this simple thing: I have in Sara a lifelong friend and sister. We made a choice to be friends, and it has proven fruitful all these years.

Of choices, Matthew Kelly writes:

"Everything is a choice. This is life's greatest truth and its hardest lesson. It is a great truth because it reminds us of our power. Not power over others, but the often untapped power to be ourselves and to live the life we have imagined. It is a hard lesson, because it causes us to realize that we have chosen the life we are living right now. It is perhaps fright-ening for us to think that we have chosen to live our life exactly as it is today. Frightening because we may not like what we find when we look at our lives today. But it is also liberating, because we can now begin to choose what we will find when we look at our life in the tomorrows that lie unlived before us."

Why am I sharing this quote? Because I realize that even with friendships, how we choose them is really critical. Isn't it our choice to buy the kind of girdle that we want based on how it fits us? You can go with a friend to help you decide, but at the end of the day, you are the one to make that final decision. The same is true for choosing friends.

Chapter 3
THE RIGHT STYLE

"But what is the good of friendship if one cannot say exactly what one means? Anybody can say charming things and try to please and to flatter, but a true friend always says unpleasant things, and does not mind giving pain. Indeed, if he is a really true friend he prefers it, for he knows that then he is doing good."

Oscar Wilde

Setting the Stage: "I realized that if I wanted to keep my sanity and not let others define me, there was only one thing I could do, and that was to have faith in God's plan for me." These words came from First Lady Michelle Obama as she addressed the Tuskegee University graduating class of 2015.

She shared her deepest concerns of what others would think of her as the first African American First Lady: "Potentially the first African American First Lady, I was also the focus of another set of questions and speculations; conversations sometimes rooted in the fears and misperceptions of others, was I too loud, or too angry, or too emasculating?" she said, addressing some of the stereotypes of black women.

As I listened to her speech, I was reminded that each one of us goes into relationships with some form of fears and misperceptions. Until we are willing to learn about someone else and develop meaningful relationships, it is safe to assume that our misperceptions will prevail. We consciously or subconsciously refuse to accept people for who they really are. We want to "control" them so that they can cater to our own insecurities and fears.

Oscar Wilde's quote makes me smile because I have had friends who have been honest with me, even when their honesty was painful. What was comforting though, was realizing that their intentions were from a place of love. On the flip side of this coin, we may have friends who come at us from a place of insecurity, anger, or jealousy. Therefore, their "honesty" in addressing an issue with us is suspect. We have to be discerning when it comes to the issues of honest communication.

God has made us all unique, and that is what makes us all beautiful. And in our uniqueness, we all have different tastes in everything, be it clothes, music, or food. When I go to shop for a girdle, I cannot have another person's shape in mind for my fitting. I need to take my body into the fitting room and try on a girdle that will fit my body shape. Sometimes we go into relationships wanting to fit a size that is not complementary to our fit. In our brokenness, we are looking to fit into a particular size instead of finding what fits us.

The key to knowing your style, in no particular order, is being familiar with the basics. What is your favorite color of girdle? Do you want a full-body girdle or just for the thigh area? Then you think of your height, your weight, your body shape (hourglass, oval, rectangle, etc.), and all things external! After you have done all that, you go to the store, and when you see something you like, you try it on, and when it fits right, it's a keeper. However, when it doesn't, it's on to the next thing.

Girlfriend "H.'s" Story: I suppose I'm showing my age here, but when I hear the word girdle, I think of my mother and my grandmother saying, "I need to get home and get out of this girdle." I don't think body-shaper, I don't mean smoother. I mean girdle, from the root word "gird" which means to cinch or bind with a belt or band, to surround; enclose; and hem in, to brace, steel, or fortify.

We know the benefit of a good girdle, but despite all that is great about them, anyone who has worn one knows they are uncomfortable. Any woman to don one knows going in, or soon after, that you must endure the discomfort in order to reap its benefits. There is so much comfort that is promised and delivered in the Scriptures, but there's much that brings me discomfort, too.

My case in point: Proverbs 27:6. *"Faithful are the wounds of a friend, but the kisses of an enemy are deceitful."* That's not right...that can't be right! Surely he meant faithful are kisses of a friend and the wounds of an enemy are deceitful. You know, Solomon had his off days...it is well documented that Solomon loved him some wine (see Ecclesiastes) and loved him some women (see I Kings 11). And many a man have been bemused and befuddled by one, the other or both.

But no, much to my consternation and chagrin, that was no typo (not that Solomon actually typed the Proverbs). And it took several years' hindsight for me to appreciate a wound from a friend because I much preferred the kisses of the enemy.

That was then...

I'm an ample woman, and I say that taking full advantage of vocabulary and thirty-plus years of self-confidence in the making; because, the fact is, I was a fat kid and a fat teen. Boys didn't like me and family members teased and insulted me. Being the youngest of six girls, I observed what it was like when boys liked you, but I didn't experience it.

Not until I was twenty-two did I have my first boyfriend, who was as skinny as I was fat. When I stood to his left, we looked like the number ten. I was happy for a while because I finally had a boyfriend, but it didn't take long for me to learn that this boyfriend stuff was not all that it was cracked up to be . I started to think that something had to be wrong with any man that wanted to be with me. I wasn't thin, I wasn't pretty, I wasn't sexy, and I wasn't good at relationships. Who would want that?!

But then I got saved, and I became fixated on the idea that God had a man for me—a good man, a Christian who accepted

THE RIGHT STYLE

me, who was drawn to my heart more than my body. He'd thoroughly love me for all of me; not a hottie, not a body, but me for me. Ten years later, and I still hadn't met him. Instead of hopeful, I was dismayed. I came to the conclusion that he didn't exist.

I spent years praying for God to make this guy love me or make that guy see me. When those things didn't happen, I came back to where I started…I'm not thin enough, I'm not pretty enough, I'm not sexy enough and apparently, as a Christian, not Proverbs 31 enough for a husband. Not even God could make a man want me.

After years of crying, fasting, praying and dreaming about the "man of God" for me, I was done. So, I made a decision that I'm ashamed to admit. In fact, I even said it out loud: "I'm not getting a husband…I just want a fling." And two days after making that statement, as if on cue, I ran into *him*. I'd known this man for over fifteen years. He was the kind of good-looking that made grown women giggle. He was that fine that you pronounced with two syllables (gurrlll…he is fiiiiii-yinnn or fiiiii-nah). And he wanted me. Let me repeat that…I don't think you're picking up on the impact…*he* wanted *me*!

He called when he said he'd call. He'd text if he was going to be late or couldn't make it. He'd tell me about his day (without me asking), he'd ask me what I thought about things. When I answered the phone, he'd say, "Hey, beautiful". He was a Christian. He'd ask me to pray for him, we talked about scripture and sermons; oh he's the one, right? Yeah, he was all that (not the corny, played out "alldat"); he was all that I wanted. He was the first man to look me in my eyes and call me beautiful. *And* he was married.

I was deceived by the kisses of an enemy. His kisses weren't the kisses of the enemy; my justifications and excuses were the kisses of the enemy. "He's unhappily married," "he's separated," "she's not good to him," and "he deserves to be happy." I had a CD with Gladys Knight's "If I Were Your Woman" in my car, and I had that song on repeat. I would sing over and over with Gladys, "You're like a diamond, but she treats you like glass..." I was good to him...she didn't respect him. She didn't treasure him, she didn't appreciate him; I did. I relished in the kisses of an enemy.

When the affair came to an end, I was devastated. I loved him. I cried and cried and cried, daily. I talked about it with a select few people until one friend leveled me...wounded me to my very core. She said, "He's been cheating on his wife for as long as he's been married. He preys on women with no self-esteem. You think you're different? You're not. What attracted him to you is your low self-worth. You're nothing special. He's a predator and you're a victim. Your self-worth is in the toilet."

I thought I was devastated before; I felt completely decimated then. I went to her when I was down. I knew how wrong I was; I didn't want her to tell me *I* was right. I wanted her to tell me I was going to be alright. There was never any doubt that I was doing wrong. I wanted her to support me, hug me. I wanted her to pray for me, embrace me, and inspire me; but she didn't. I wanted a kiss from my friend; but instead she wounded me, grievously so. I thought I'd never recover.

This is now...

See, hindsight isn't twenty-twenty; hindsight is clairvoyant. Hindsight knows the future. The book of Ecclesiastes was written in hindsight. It is in hindsight that we recognize a wound to be faithful. Now, I'm grateful for the friend that wounded me. At the time, I was just hurt. I was so looking for self-justification and self-righteousness that I scoffed at faithful discomfort from a friend.

We need to appreciate uncomfortable truth that reins us in when we get high and mighty. In II Samuel chapter 12, Nathan confronts David about his affair with Bathsheba and the murder of her husband. He tells David a story about a wealthy man who'd taken a poor man's ewe. King David was indignant! "I swear by the living God…any man who would do such a thing like that should be put to death!" (TLB). (At least my friend didn't tell me I should die!) He began declaring how this wealthy man ought to pay to the poor man, and then Nathan got "girdle" on him; he made it uncomfortable for David. "*You* are that rich man!" Have you ever seen someone or yourself been caught talking about a person who walks in the room or is standing behind you? So uncomfortable, so embarrassing. Taking a harsh and judgmental stance on something is deceptively easy until you realize you're the guilty party.

So how does a wound become faithful? It depends on how you handle it. David could have arranged for Nathan's death. But (v. 13) "David said to Nathan, I have sinned against the Lord." Nathan's harsh words hemmed him in, and David turned to God. That's how a wound is faithful; we stop self-justifying, let go of our self-righteousness, and turn to God. And Nathan tells David "the Lord has put away your sin."

My sisters, let's take full advantage of hindsight; be forgiving and appreciative of a wound from a friend. Don't let discomfort be the reason to dismiss and discard a friendship. Like a good girdle, it's tight but it's right…in fact, it's right because it's tight. We all need a good girlfriend who is like a girdle—TIGHT—sometimes to the point of discomfort—but who reins you in when you're high and mighty, holds you together and does not allow things to fall out.

Girdle Guidelines: "H's" story is a reminder of friendships that help you "come to your senses." In order to be that friend (one who is firm, honest and full of grace), we need to consider the following:

- Who you are: Know what makes you uniquely you and don't compromise your core values.
- You must accept your friends in their form, but be willing to grow together.
- Communicate with grace and truth. Always pray before discussing tough conversations.
- Season your conversion with love, grace and truth!

There should be relational capital and safety (and not judgment) when it comes to conversations with friends. In the parting words of Brené Brown, you don't need a friend "who needs you to be the pillar of worthiness and authenticity. She can't help because she is too disappointed in your imperfections. You've let her down. The friend who is so uncomfortable with vulnerability that she scolds you: 'How did you let this happen?'"

The Last Word: *"We allow our ignorance to prevail upon us and make us think we can survive alone, alone in patches, alone in groups, alone in races, even alone in genders."*

Maya Angelou

Chapter 4
Try It on First

"If friends disappoint you over and over, that's in large part your own fault. Once someone has shown a tendency to be self-centered, you need to recognize that and take care of yourself; people aren't going to change simply because you want them to."

Oprah Winfrey

Setting the Stage: I have heard it said in so many different forms that frustration is the gap between reality and expectations. Our biggest source of angst in our lives with regards to friendship is when we expect one thing, and we get the other in return. We need to face the reality that not all friendships give us the same results, hence the need to know exactly who we are dealing with, consistently.

We need to try on our friendships as we try on our shapewear before we commit to making that purchase. According to an article on the "Dos and Don'ts of Wearing Shapewear," "Every woman has a different body and different preferences, and just because a friend raves about her control brief does not mean it is great for everyone. The only way to be sure a body shaper works is to put it on and see how it looks underneath clothing."

Just because other friendships work for your friends does not necessarily mean they will work for you. Be willing to be inconvenienced sometimes to go the extra mile and try on that friendship or shapewear before it becomes a source of frustration.

Girlfriend "S.'s" Story: In the course of life, I have learned that there will be many occasions to determine how strong or weak your ability is to handle the most tumultuous situations. It is in these times that life can explode with ever increasing questions of how mature, relevant, and powerful you are or are not. Sometimes we come to the places during these seasons of life that, no matter how hard we try, we just can't see past the pain we are experiencing or the obstacles that seem to be in our way.

It has been in these times in my own life that the tightening belt that held me together has been that of my closest friends. My girdle girls. As a woman, I am learning that there are words that I can only speak about to one of these special friends in my life. I have had more than one occasion to be in a relationship with a man. Men, I have learned, are as dynamic as their female counterparts. But, one of the things that make a man is the blatant reality that they want to solve EVERYTHING. They don't tend to want you to keep talking but, at the end of the day, they want you, as a woman, to say what you need to say as quickly as possible. They just want it to be fixed and then simply...it's done.

Oh, how many stories can I tell of my many relationships in which I was *feeling* a certain way and just wanted to express what I was *feeling* to the man that was in my life. It never failed that, before long, after just a few, if not one of these conversations, somehow frustration or just complete confusion would appear on my man's face.

I spent countless days, weeks, and months not understanding why it was that every time I entered a relationship with a man they never *understood* me. After all, shouldn't a man that wanted me in his life know what I was talking about when I went from this point, back to that point, and then made a new point within five minutes? Was there just something wrong with me, or were the men I was dealing with a little bit slow?

Well, truth be told it was a little bit of both but, as I have learned more recently in my life, it is because I never understood the simplest truth since Adam and Eve. THEY are from Mars, and WE are from Venus—we are totally not the same. Simple truth but, once again, this very feminine brain of mine could not capture that very simple reality.

All that said, I started realizing that if I really wanted to be understood fully, or maybe not even understood, but just to have someone listen for as long as I wanted to rattle without fixing anything, I would find it in my girdle girls. In many ways what I am about to say sounds a bit funny, but I realized that maybe I couldn't talk to the men in my life because most of my problems have been about them. So it only makes sense that it has been my girdle girlfriends whom I leaned on the most in times of great anxiety.

That's not to say that I only talk to the women of my life about men problems, but that is the beauty of having these type of women surrounding you. It really never matters what you talk about. It could be beautiful, sad, frightening, or just a normal day and, because of the bond, love and care you share for your sister-girl, you really don't care. All you know is that they are there for you, and you are there for them.

I have been beyond blessed to have around ten women in my life like this, most of whom have been there for at least the last ten years. It is an extraordinary thing to be surrounded by not just professional, Godly women who know who they are, but women who know the importance of friendship.

Girdle Guidelines: Online shopping has become one of the easiest ways to shop. You don't have to fight the crowds or traffic to get to the mall. With a click on your smartphone, tablet, or computer, you are able to buy exactly what you need. However, with shapewear, sometimes it becomes tricky because of its specific function and how it needs to fit your specific body type.

The same can be said about friendships—what function they play in our lives and which friendships fit in our moments of need. As we navigate through the process of finding meaningful relationships and "trying them on" first, one of the things we come across is finding out if we share the same interests, values, and convictions. Some of the most critical questions we need to ask ourselves as we try on these friendships are the following:

- Do we share the same values intellectually?
- Do we share the same values spiritually?
- Do we share the same values emotionally?
- Do we share the same values socially?
- Do you feel safe emotionally, psychologically, mentally with this person?

As we intensely look at these questions and use them as a barometer to connect and find meaningful friendships, we will realize sooner than later that some relationships are not the right fit. They may feel okay at first try but, the longer you stay in them, the more you realize they are uncomfortable and dysfunctional for you. Tim A. Gardner in his book, "The Naked Soul," says it best. "Feeling pressured to have friends forces you into artificial relationships and always leads to frustration. You're searching for a friend who truly knows you and loves you no matter what. Those friends are never found in the compulsive, superficial relationships of pressured friendships."

The Last Word: *"Have convictions; be friendly; stick to your beliefs as they stick to theirs; work as hard as they do. Friendship with one's self is all important, because without it one cannot be friends with anyone else in the world."*

Eleanor Roosevelt

Chapter 5
Fit Matters

"One friend with whom you have a lot in common is better than three with whom you struggle to find things to talk about. We never needed best friend gear because I guess with real friends you don't have to make it official. It just is."

Mindy Kaling

Setting the Stage: I remember a story Octavia Spencer, who won a Screen Actors Guild award (SAG) for her supporting role in *The Help*, told about her shapewear. On The Ellen DeGeneres Show, Spencer admitted to wearing three pairs of Spanx at the SAG awards and how she "could not party that night because I was being pinched in places I didn't know it was possible."

It so happens that Melissa McCarthy was also having the same struggle with her shapewear. For Melissa, she had the courage to go to the bathroom and take hers off after Spencer admitted, "Melissa, I'm about to die. My Spanx are killing me." Melissa probably felt the same way Spencer felt, but she chose to be pain-free and enjoy the party at the expense of being criticized for her "looks."

We know Hollywood is unforgiving when it comes to how women look, but kudos to McCarthy and Spencer for admitting that what they were wearing was not working for them. It was causing more pain than the results they were looking for. Ever had a "friend" who sacked the living daylights out of you because they are not a good fit? They squeeze you so tight, you can barely breathe most times! HA!

Girlfriend "N.'s" Story: In sitting down to share a relationship story, I have been challenged beyond words. Originally, I picked a situation with a friend that was easy to tell. The story was simple. We didn't fit each other anymore. There is no drama. Life has moved on, and I'm ok with it. Then I thought about the intent of this book. I read back over the vision and expectations the author and dear friend stated, and I knew the story I told had to be a deeper and more transparent one. Here we go!

I am a thirty-five-year-old single Christian woman. I have never been married. I love the Lord. I was raised in a family of believers who passionately love the Lord as well. For as long as I can remember, what I have wanted to be is a wife and a mother. It was my full desire and intention to remain a virgin until I was married. If I did so, surely I deserved what I wanted. I did just that until I turned thirty-four. You may say thirty-four!? Why such a compromise after waiting for so long? And that brings us to my Girdle Girlfriend story.

She's an amazing woman. She doesn't criticize me. She listens for the true intent behind my words. She pays attention to the meaning behind my actions. She knows me, in some areas, possibly better than I know myself. She looks at me and sees who I truly am, not the image I worked so hard to maintain over the years. She was one of the only people I felt I could go to with what I had done.

I was crushed. I was broken. I was suffering in shame, guilt, and regret. There are so many reasons, not excuses, that this compromise occurred that God has allowed me to see through conversations with my dear friend and sister. She heard my heart. She validated my feelings. She picked me up with her love so that I could keep pushing forward. She did not allow me to stay in a defeated place.

However, I did remain in a place of embarrassment and shame. She is still only one of two friends who knows about this incident in my life. You see, I could not let people know that I was that flawed. I couldn't let on that I was that weak. I had to continue the façade that I had it all together. I was the good girl, and it had to stay that way. I was not challenged in this area again until one year later.

I met a man who I believe to be the most significant earthly male in my life other than my father. I adore him. I promised myself and the Lord that I was waiting until marriage. However, recently, I had sex with a man who is not yet my husband. This time, there was more of a rawness to how I felt. It wasn't really guilt or shame at first.

I pulled away to spend some time with the Lord. I was crying out to Him in desperation. Why Lord? Why am I doing this? This is not who I am. This was not supposed to be. I was broken. Finally broken enough for God to shed light on something I had been covering up.

After this intense time of worship, I called my dear sister friend. She listened to me. She heard my heart. She heard the condemnation. She called it out just as I had done for her in times past. As she did this, God began to show me clear as day that I had been a virgin for so long in my own strength.

It was me striving to be the perfect Christian girl so that I could deserve the perfect Christian man. It was not because I was trying to honor God with my body. It was not because I had such a fear and reverence for the Lord. It was so that I could say I did it right. Now give me what I deserve. It was all about me. And I had reached a place where "ME" had run out.

God was showing me that being a wife had become an idol in my heart. He was showing me that I was not relying on Him for the gift of a husband. I was relying on "ME" to get that husband by doing everything the right way. My friend listened as these revelations from the Lord came pouring out of my mouth. I was shocked. It was ugly. It was painful to see my flaws. However, I felt safe to see them with her.

Ladies, when thinking about Girdle Girlfriends, this is something you need to keep at the forefront of your mind: can you be completely transparent with her and still feel safe? If you can't, then she may not fit you. The author of this book states, "The most important key element to remember is that if the girdle is not comfortable, then it does not fit you." This is crucial.

You are going to go through some trying and uncomfortable situations. You should have those few girlfriends in your life who you are comfortable walking through those uncomfortable situations with. You need to be able to dig into the depths of who you are with a girdle type girlfriend. Let's be real ladies; transparency is where the growth, learning, and healing take place. It's not comfortable, but you can be comfortable with a Girdle Girlfriend in the uncomfortable places."

Girdle Guidelines: When my friend shared her experience with me, I could hear the pain in her voice and the regret and how she probably struggled to tell me about this part of her journey. Yet, through this discomfort, she felt she could share her deepest hurt because we are a "good fit." We had enough relational capital between us that being vulnerable with each other was somewhat a no-brainer. The things that can possibly determine this level of a good fit and vulnerability along the friendship journey are the following:

- Can they can handle your flaws? *If they cannot accept you for you and your flaws, it's a good indication they are not a good fit.*

- Do they challenge you to be a better person physically, emotionally, spiritually, mentality, financially?

- Do they work with you through miscommunications and fears? Fear is a killer of all relationships, but if we are willing to work through them, we are bound to succeed.

- Your gut instincts: sometimes you just know that the relationship you are hoping to form is just not going to work. Your instincts are a form of convictions—listen to them.

In concluding this chapter, I will share one final thought from Tim A. Gardner on being holistic. "Authentic relationships require both deep intimacy and clearly defined individuality. In other words, being intimately connected to another person works only if you are self-aware and an emotionally healthy individual. Connected yet fully independent. That's the key." As we continue to find healthy relationships, may it be our personal goal to be healthy individuals; where we are at peace in our hearts, not associated with drama and not creating drama either. It's only when we are healthy individuals that we can be a good fit for others or vice versa.

The Last Word: *"Vulnerability is the birthplace of connection and the path to the feeling of worthiness. If it doesn't feel vulnerable, the sharing is probably not constructive."*

Brené Brown

Benefits of Wearing Girdles

Watching old Victorian movies made me cringe when I would see the ladies with their little umbrellas walking in the park with their long dresses that seemed to squeeze their midsection. I couldn't, and still cannot, imagine myself in those dresses. However, truth be told, there are benefits to wearing girdles, such as improving one's posture and confidence and helping with unwanted bulges, to mention a few. In the following chapters, let us consider some benefits of shapewear and friendships.

Chapter 6
IMPROVES YOUR POSTURE

"Nothing makes a woman more beautiful than the belief that she is beautiful!"

Sophia Loren

Setting The Stage: Anne Harding, a writer for Health Magazine, states that, "Good posture will do more to keep you looking youthful as the years go by than a facelift or Botox. And the benefits of maintaining your bone health are much more than skin-deep." Recommendations are given on how to control having great posture as you age, anywhere from doing Pilates, to lifting weights, to sitting up straight without slouching your back. It is also known that having a bad posture can cause, not only emotional problems like depression but also bodily harm.

BENEFITS OF GIRDLES

"Slouching also causes your body to compress and constrict. When in this position, your heart and lungs are forced to work harder to pump blood and circulate oxygen. This causes undue stress on your internal organs and your muscles. Sitting in an upright position with your shoulders and chest broad makes it easier to breathe." Therefore, one can safely say that maintaining the right posture is not only critical for your physical health but also your emotional well-being.

A girdle also helps with good posture, according to Healthable.org. "Those panty girdles that reach up the back just a little bit can provide lumbar support and may prevent back injuries. [...] An undergarment that encourages good posture has the potential of reducing, not only back injuries, but the following: headaches and migraines [...] tension in the neck and shoulders."

Girlfriend "A.'s" Story: The "internist," that's the nickname that my girdle girlfriend Tanya bestowed upon me a few years into our now eighteen-year friendship. While an internist, by definition, is a physician who practices internal medicine, Tanya facetiously used the term to define me as someone who practiced keeping my feelings and personal business on the inside. She couldn't have been more accurate in her assessment of me.

You see, I was raised by a loving, yet super protective and well-meaning, mother who taught me from an early age not to trust everybody, especially females. I was advised not to tell females my business because they were jealous and catty. Growing up I didn't have a lot of girlfriends and the ones I did have, I only told them things on a need-to-know basis. My mother was my confidant, and I cherished our relationship and talks so much that I felt like I didn't need female friends.

By the time I arrived at college, I had mastered the art of privacy. When Tanya and I met during our sophomore year of college, I found her to be confident, approachable, nice, and open. I noticed right away that we were very different. She was outgoing and, of course, I was introverted. She kept things real and actually made me feel like I was one of her sisters more than a friend. As our friendship evolved, I discovered that she was not only trustworthy, but she didn't strike me as being jealous. Tanya shared things with me that, to this day, I've never repeated. Even though she was that person to me, for some reason, I just didn't feel like I could be as open with her. Keeping my feelings bottled up and my business to myself was very intentional, and when I needed to talk, I simply called my mom.

Tanya always knew when I was going through something or was purposely keeping things from her and would just let me know to call her when I was ready to talk. By the time I would call her, she would ascertain whether or not I was alright and then proceed to tell me about her day, her boyfriend, and anything else that was going on with her. We continued on this way all the way through school.

The year that we graduated from college, Tanya began attending church and eventually re-dedicated her life to Jesus Christ. Her relationship was growing with the Lord, we both were starting new jobs, and we were both dating people. Things seemed to be going well for both of us, and while she had made me very much a part of her life, I still hadn't fully made her a part of mine. All of that changed the following year when I found out that I was pregnant.

It's no surprise that I hadn't told Tanya much about the guy that I was dating, and she never met him. So when I called her to say I was pregnant, needless to say, she was stunned. She was even more stunned by my abrupt and poorly thought out decision to move back home to Virginia to deal with this with my family at my side. I was disappointed in myself, scared, and did not want to be a single mother. Tanya assured me that she was there for me and called regularly to check on me after I relocated.

Very early in the pregnancy, I suffered a miscarriage, and my doctor told me that I would go through a grieving process. I was unprepared, at best, for the deep depression that followed and lasted a year. Although I had opened up to Tanya about my pregnancy and subsequent miscarriage, the depression I suffered drastically challenged our friendship.

Whenever she called me, I could hear my mother telling her that I was asleep, even if it was 2:00 pm. I stayed in bed day and night only getting up to use the bathroom and eat a little. When I was able to muster up enough strength to talk to her, I barely made a sound as it required too much effort to hold a conversation.

Things got so bad that, as Tanya called more frequently, all I could do was listen. I felt like I had let my family down and I wanted to die. Being the consistent and instinctive friend that she was, Tanya continued to call, assuring me that I didn't have to say anything and that she loved me, was praying for me, and that I would be ok.

Somewhere during that dark time, I made my way to church with my mom, received Christ as my savior and began opening up to God. I literally cried out so hard to the Lord that I felt like I was dying because my body hurt so much from crying. During those moments, God showed me that Tanya was not only a friend to me but a sister. He showed me that I needed her in my life and reminded me of how she remained a friend to me even though she didn't know nearly as much about me as I knew about her. God allowed me to see that He placed us in each other's lives and that she is someone whom I can trust and talk to.

My mom, who had once discouraged me from trusting women, came to love and trust Tanya like another daughter. When my mom was dying of breast cancer in 2005, she encouraged me to call Tanya and talk to her about what *I* was going through. While lifting my spirits, my friend also leaned on me for support as she and her husband were expecting their first child, she had lost an aunt, and she learned that her father was also terminally ill.

By sharing my heartfelt feelings of what it felt like watching my mom slipping away, I think it helped Tanya to have someone to relate to what she was going through. Opening up my feelings with her allowed me to create a common ground between us and made it easier for us to lean on each other. When she lost her dad a month after I lost my mom, we talked at great length about our feelings and how thankful we were that God had placed us in each other's lives. Today, there's nothing that I don't share with my friend.

Having a girdle girlfriend like Tanya taught me how to be a friend. From the very beginning, she tailored our friendship to be a safe, nurturing, and comforting place. For eighteen years she has never once wavered in her friendship with me. My friend, by her own example, holds the distinction of single-handedly dispelling the myth I had about women since childhood. Her genuine support of me makes me stand tall, feel loved, and strive to be the friend to her that she has been to me. My "internist" side still shows up sometimes when I'm stressed and when it does my girdle girlfriend tightens up, keeps me in check, and tells me to call her when I "feel better"!

Girdle Guidelines: Reading "A's" story makes me think about the power of choice. Based on her upbringing, "A" was taught not to trust another female and, therefore, kept herself guarded. The posture of lack of trust had her slouched over unable to find a safe place to unload the dealings of life. On the other hand, Tanya also made a choice. She had a posture of openness and trust. She accepted "A" and extended her friendship to her. Over time, "A" chose to trust Tanya because she (Tanya), had deposited enough relational capital into her life that it was okay to trust. Gary Smalley shares that, "choice equals change. Making a choice is often difficult because it requires change. And that change can be threatening."

For "A" to choose to open up her heart and to trust Tanya meant she would leave the past behind and venture on to a better future. Their "posture" made it possible for their friendship to remain through it all. Positive posture in friendships gives us the following traits:

- **Self Confidence**: Think of the time when you thought you couldn't do something and talking to one of your closest friends made you believe you could do the task.
- **A Sense of Belonging**: When you know that you have been embraced by someone without a sense of judgment, it gives you a sense of belonging, a sense of family, and a sense of acceptance.
- **Mental Fortitude**: When your friends fight with you and for you during life challenges, you mentally become strong and are more willing to fight and overcome the battle.
- **A Sounding Board**: Having a girdle friend to reel you back in and help you see things objectively helps you in the long run. A friend who is even-keeled in your moments of insanity is needed at all times.

The opposite is true if we have friends who are nothing but drama. They bring baggage into our lives, which in turn causes stress, high blood pressure, and tension to mention but a few. They give us a bad posture. I Corinthians 15:33 states, "Bad company corrupts good morals." God never created us to have bad posture by having toxic relationships. Let's be intentional in building healthy relationships that will improve our posture.

> The Last Word: *"The best relationships in our lives are the best not because they have been the happiest ones, they are that way because they have stayed strong through the most tormentful of storms."*
>
> Pandora Poikilos

Chapter 7
You Move Freely

"Let not others define you, make yourself strong and able to define yourself. When you accept yourself with your worthiness and weakness, you are invincible."

Dr. Anil Kr Sinha

Setting The Stage: "I've learned now that, sometimes, letting go can be the best way to be a good friend." I came across the statement when reading an article in The Huffington Post by Annabelle Gurwitch, *"The Words That Cost Me My Most Important Friendship."* The statement made me stop in my tracks because it was just an honest statement, yet a hurtful reality when you consider that she was in this friendship for more than thirty years and one phone call changed the dynamics of this friendship. I was grateful that Annabelle took responsibility for what led up to this breakup. It helps one, when moving forward, to decide not to repeat the same mistakes.

I cringed at this story because I am a sucker for relationships. I want everyone to get along, I want ALL relationships to work; I believe in the gifts of reconciliation, forgiveness, patience, etc. However, that is not reality. Relationships sometimes are beyond repair, can be tricky and at times complicated.

Girlfriend "T.'s" Story: I gave my life to Christ in college, and before that, *all* of my relationships were bad! I believe I could mark this friendship as the first godly friendship I had. I saw in her qualities I desired for myself. I saw in her values I felt were just like mine. I believed God ordained this relationship. We both seemed to witness God confirming this to be a friendship He'd begun. We didn't rush into the friendship or take each other for granted but developed what I would call a close friendship. She was my best friend.

I felt *free* in the relationship. Free to be *me* (in the beginning) and believed she did, too.

I saw her as *wise*, and I felt *valued* by her. That changed when I began to notice that she rarely included me in group settings. Later, she made a comment about my being "classy" and that she felt comfortable having me around her other friends. (Okay. I felt the same way about her; no big deal.) I noticed after a while that she began introducing me to her other close friends and including me in group settings. All went well.

Later, she told me a comment that a family member made to her concerning me: "She's not your pet project, you know?" (Huh? What was that about?) I just stuck that one on the back burner for the time being. Well, later there were a couple of times when I had begun to feel just that—like she wanted to groom me in some way. She would even try to "primp" me at times. I thought, "Was I *that* bad? I thought you said I was *already* classy!" This was not the type of relationship I wanted to have. Still, I let it go.

At one point after our friendship was established, I'd been looking for an opportunity to dance. It had been a long time since I'd been able to dance. My background was performing arts, and I was itching to do something that glorified God. My girlfriend and I were talking on the phone one evening (as usual) and I mentioned it to her. Well, she told me there just happened to be auditions for a string of musicals being produced at a local Christian theatre. She also happened to have participated in this seasonal production in the past and just happened to be auditioning again herself. She volunteered to take me to the auditions. Great, right? Wrong. I had a bad feeling about her taking me to these auditions—that "pet project" feeling. I wanted this to be something I did on my own. I was an adult, and I could take myself to the auditions, thank you! (But why didn't I just tell her that? I didn't want to be introduced into this new environment as her "pet friend." Ugghh!)

The rehearsals were going well, but she was the choreographer for one of the pieces, and I began to feel more like I had a new boss than a friend. Mind you, not only was I a Christian, but I was a semi-professional, so I bit my lip, forgave a lot, and moved on because this was "part of the business," though I started to feel that my girlfriend and I might not be close friends after this was over.

I could usually pick up on a move quickly and perfect it, but one part of the choreography became very challenging for me. I was the only one not getting this *one* step. It was a very vulnerable feeling. I was frustrated with myself, and I could tell others were growing impatient. I felt very self-conscious and embarrassed.

Due to time constraints, I suggested we move on and I'd practice the move outside of rehearsal, attempting to reassure everyone that "I'd get the move down" in time for the show. Well, apparently my girlfriend/choreographer didn't like my suggestion. I suddenly had the feeling that she thought this was about her (*again*). To my surprise, she wags her finger back and forth while telling me to "C-o-m-e h-e-r-e!" Not loud, just very bossy! (Excuse me?)

I looked at everyone's faces, and they were wide-eyed and stunned. (Okay, so it's not just me.) Again she wags her finger and points down to the area of the stage near her feet, rolls her eyes and forms a drawl in her voice saying, again, "C-o-m-e h-e-r-e! Over here. Right h-e-r-e." Again, not loud, just very *bossy!* I bit my lip and swallowed the two *drops* of pride I had left (and you could hear the *gulp*).

I walked over to her and did her bidding. She then went on to say how she was in charge…yada yada yada. (Whew! Help me, Jesus!) I said to myself, "this will NEVER happen again." A few days later, we talked, and I tried to help her understand how this, among other things, made me feel. She seemed to feel like *I* embarrassed *her*. *She* brought me to these auditions to meet the people in *her* circle and on and on. I could not believe I was hearing this power trip! It was all about her! The relationship seemed to stall for a while.

Some time had passed, and our relationship seemed to pick up again, though not with the same fervor and vigor. I was searching for a new church home (something I had not anticipated) and was desperate for godly fellowship and spiritual support. It was a hard time, and she had been aware of the problems I'd been facing. We'd helped each other through many hard times. My girlfriend (being a friend) invited me to a cell group meeting she had been attending, where I was very honest about the issue I was facing and that I needed help with it.

On the ride home, my friend told me (again) how embarrassed I'd made her feel when discussing my issue. I thought to myself, "This isn't about you! I'm the one who needs help here, and you're so concerned with your *image* that you can't see that I'm *bleeding* here!"

I knew I couldn't let this issue go any further awry. We made a stop on the way home, and I managed to calmly tell her how I was feeling—all the while not wanting her to be upset with me. But she stormed out of the car. She didn't even want to address it! It didn't go well. On top of that, there were already some unspoken feelings and concerns leftover from the previous conflict. I tried to reason with her but couldn't. There was just awkward silence the rest of the ride home.

It just seemed to go downhill from there. I was left to believe that this person I had so much respect for, had invested so much of myself in (and who had seemingly invested so much into me), really did not care for me to the degree I'd once believed. I just couldn't deal with someone who so obviously no longer valued me—if she ever really did.

I do want to address what I believe to be my own failings in the relationship with my girlfriend. First, I should have paid attention to what I was seeing and hearing and addressed it at that time. My desire to avoid conflict to the degree that I didn't address the issue immediately was due to my fear of losing the friendship.

Also, while I believe I addressed my friend in love, I know that I certainly may have come across unloving in my communication. We may have been able to work through our misunderstandings earlier, had I not been so fearful and angry—a very frustrating combination. I thought I was fighting for the relationship when I was actually crippling it by not addressing issues timely.

It does not automatically follow that when we disagree we also have to part, but we often do. When I did sense God nudging me to reconcile with her a few years later, I was so fearful of being rejected that I never reached out to her. For all I know, it could have just as well been for her benefit as for mine. I did contact her some years later on the eve of her wedding and a move across country to start a new job. I wished her well and was truly happy for her, knowing some of what she had come through to get to that day.

Girdle Guidelines: So much can be pulled from this story, and most of you can draw your conclusion and see yourself as the friend (if you are willing to be honest) or the "pet friend." What we are discussing is moving freely in a friendship by accepting each other for who we are and our imperfections. We also need to challenge each other to grow and become soul healthy. By soul healthy, I mean that you as an individual are emotionally, spiritually, and socially healthy. You can love easily because you love yourself. You can forgive easily, because you forgive yourself. You can accept easily, because you accept yourself.

During a women's conference I attended, the question "Why don't women get along?" was asked. One of the panel speakers, Lydia Osborne gave us some perspective. She said, paraphrased, that if we fail to love ourselves, we take our issues into all relationships. This breeds disconnection in relationships. The simple reason is *we are projecting our lack of self-love on others.*

I thought that was a powerful assessment. I came across a quote on Twitter by @InspowerMinds stating, "If someone has something bad to say about you, it's probably because they have nothing good to say about themselves." Granted, people will say good things about themselves but, if truth be told, we are a true reflection of how we treat others, good or bad.

Below are some of the ways one can know if they are moving freely in their relationships or if these friendships have become toxic:

- When you begin to compromise your core values. You realize you are not happy with the person you are becoming in the relationship.

- When apologies are met with justification as to why they did what they did without really being sorry.

- When the person does not build you up but breaks you

down because they want to be the center of attention.

- They are not happy when you are succeeding. They want you to stay broken and to struggle through life.

- When they can lie to your face, and you know it.

The list is endless. It goes beyond these five points. There are online articles, magazines, and books that will give you a comprehensive list of toxic signs in relationships. The only caution I advise is to check yourself first to find out if you are toxic before you begin to point the finger at others.

> **The Last Word:** *"It's easy to say we love others but difficult to allow them the freedom inherent in love. We withdraw, feel resentful, send guilt messages and attempt to control those who do things against our wishes. These actions kill freedom and will, and they eventually kill love. Love cannot exist without freedom, and freedom cannot exist without responsibility. We must own and take responsibility for what is ours, and that includes our disappointment in not getting everything we want from another person. The disappointment that comes from our loved ones exercising their freedom is our responsibility. We must deal with it. This is the only way to keep love alive."*
>
> Cloud and Townsend

Chapter 8
The Muffin Top Concealer

"I think a good friend, to me, is all about trust and loyalty. You don't ever want to second-guess whether you can tell your friend something."

Lauren Conrad

Setting the Stage: According to the Merriam-Webster dictionary, a muffin top is defined as "The fatty flesh that hangs over tightly worn pants." Most of us, with or without the tightly worn pants, still have the muffin top effect. If you surf the web, you will find tons of workouts that address how to get rid of the muffin top. Some of the suggestions include a high intensity, resistance training, cardio workout, including changing one's diet. Over time, one loses the fat around their waist if they adhere to the workout routines that work best for their body types.

However, if one hasn't begun their workout regimen to get rid of the muffin top, there is a quick solution—a girdle—that faithful friend you need when you are bulging on the edges. According to the Shape online magazine, "Spanx and other shapewear really does smooth out the body, leaving you with a clean silhouette. No muffin top, or extra skin at the bra line—it's kind of like magic."

This brings us back to how this book idea even started. Remember Pastor Janeen saying, "we need girlfriends who will act like girdles, 'holding everything tight together?'" Never letting the world see your shortcomings? That kind of friend?

Girlfriend "P.'s" Story: "Hey, I need to share something really personal, do you have time to talk?" "Sure," I said. "What's going on?"

She went on to share one of her deepest secrets and regrets with me. I could not even bring myself together after hearing what had happened. I reminisced about the times we shared life together and shared our hopes and fears, but this case was different.

In that moment, I had a choice to either accept my sister or pass judgment and condemnation. I imagined the bravery it took for her to open up her soul. You could hear the hesitation in her voice and see the tears streaming down her face as she walked through the journey that had brought her to this place. She knew she was risking it all in telling me her story. But I don't think, in that moment, she had anything to lose, other than having a clear conscious after sharing her struggle.

We talked and prayed and cried together after that, and the rest is history. Years have passed since that encounter, but never once have I shared those details with anyone, until this moment. And let me say, no further details will be shared past what has been written because I am a muffin-top concealer. I will go to my grave knowing I kept that information.

The best way to sum up the muffin top concealer can be found in a recent message I heard online by Andy Stanley, Pastor of Northpoint Church in Atlanta, Georgia titled, "The Mess in the Mirror." In it, he advocates that WE ALL are messed up, either financially, academically, socially, or whatever.

He says, "Mess is what brings us together today. Before you are critical, you need to remember that you are a mess as well. And when it comes to the people around us whose lives are messy, we should be students, not critics because when you hear someone's story behind their mess, you see them differently."

I would suggest that when we understand each other's messed up lives, we become concealers of mistakes and not revealers of them. Imagine a world where if slip-ups are shared, no one else will know about them because we realize, if tables were turned, that could be us in that situation. What is the golden rule? "Do unto others as you would have them do unto you."

I often think about the times when I have been a revealer of mistakes in the name of sharing a concern. You know how great we are at "sharing concerns" ladies! Let's call a spade a spade. We call that gossiping. I look back now and repent for not being a muffin-top concealer because I have been on the other side when what I shared with a friend in confidence was later shared with someone else.

The emotional violation I felt in that moment was so hurtful. I was able to look at the mess in the mirror of my mistakes by having it happen to me. As they say, "we reap what we sow." I turned a corner and vowed to never be the one who reveals the mistakes of others, no matter how close I am to someone, but to be the ultimate concealer of mistakes.

I have had situations where someone has come up to me to share some negative news about my friends. I have stood up for them and defended their reputation, regardless of whether I know the truth or not because my commitment is to them and not to someone trying to cause strife and division.

As our sisters' keepers, we need to begin to ask ourselves the question, "What is our motivation for bringing up these stories?" "Are we adding value to the friendship or destruction?" "Are we better off having had this conversation or have we just grieved God?" Being hurt does not give us the right to expose other people's weaknesses. But as the adage says, "Hurt people hurt people."

Girdle Guidelines: In this day and age, it is very hard to find "friends" who will not let your bulging edges be known. As women, we are quick to share a struggle another friend is experiencing with another woman, not to help, but to "talk about it." In doing so, we are exposing the muffin tops of our sisters to the "world" even if we are sharing with people we "trust." It is hard enough to open up our hearts to each other, let alone have your weaknesses be exposed. We should be keepers of our sisters at all costs.

I remember listening to a message by Dr. Dharius Daniels from Ewing, New Jersey about, "What kind of friend are you?" I highly recommend that you listen to this message. It can be found on YouTube as well as their church app, Kingdom Church. In this message, he said two things that made me think hard. He said, "We need to be a relational asset, not a liability, in the lives of friends God sends us." And then he said, "When you are a friend, and someone trusts you with their business, they trust YOU with their business. They are not trusting who you trust. So you don't have the right to share with others something that someone shared with you when they did not give you the permission to share."

Think about those two statements for a second. How many times have we done the latter in the name of, "prayer?" Yet, when we do that, we are letting our friends bulge, showing their muffin tops. We are not holding them tight so that their issues are not being exposed for the whole world to see. Therefore, the benefits of having girdle girlfriends who don't expose your muffin tops are pretty simple:

- **They are protective of the friendship**. They shut down or do not entertain conversations that only bring about drama in their lives or yours.
- **They defend the friendship**. They see the bulge, but they don't expose it to others. They work with you to be a better

person so that your flaws don't override your inner beauty.

- **They are loyal to the friendship**. These friends have your back. They don't share your secrets with others and vice-versa. Goes back to what Pastor Daniels said earlier.

You may have other qualities to add to this list, but my prayer is that we heed the words of Pastor Daniels; be an asset in someone's life and not a destructive person. Protect your friendships at all costs. Be that friend, regardless of time, situation, environment, disappointment, hurt, anger, and frustration, who doesn't talk ill of your friends. However, if we do, there is much to be said about what kind of friends we are. I will leave it up to you to draw that conclusion.

> **The Last Word:** *"Love is friendship that has caught fire. It is quiet understanding, mutual confidence, sharing and forgiving. It is loyalty through good and bad times. It settles for less than perfection and makes allowances for human weaknesses."*
>
> Ann Landers

Girdle Care

Like with any garment that you own, there are instructions that come with how to take care of them in order for them to last longer. Most times we do not read the little tag that comes with the simple instructions and we end up paying for it. The good news is: if we take the time to read the small print, we will save ourselves tons of money replacing garments.

Chapter 9
Wash on Gentle

"A friend is one to whom one may pour out all the contents of one's heart, chaff and grain together, knowing that the gentlest of hands will take and sift it, keep what is worth keeping and with a breath of kindness blow the rest away."

Arabian Proverb

Setting the Stage: Gentleness can be defined as, "the quality or state of being gentle; especially: mildness of manners or disposition." In a time when our culture deems gentleness as a weakness instead of a strength, it's no wonder we are failing to exude this powerful attribute when needed the most in friendships. The following statement best sums up the perfect picture of gentleness. "Gentleness is the virtue that restrains the passion of anger. In order to be truly gentle, one must be strong. Only strong people can be gentle because gentleness restrains strength by love. Gentleness is not an option. It is a grave obligation."

You and I can both agree that when it comes to communication and relationships, gentleness is not the first thing that crosses our minds. If anything, we view gentleness as a crippling weakness. Proverbs 15:1 says, "A gentle answer turns away wrath, but a harsh word stirs up anger." How many friendships have been destroyed because we were too quick to respond? Too quick to judge? Too quick to see things from our own dark-colored glasses? Too quick to show the passion of anger and not restraint?

Girlfriend "R.'s" Story: I perused my vast library of movies, searching for something that was "safe," that wouldn't bring her unnecessary pain. Sarah had lost two babies due to the same disease, and she wasn't yet ready to watch anything that would bring unhappy reminders of what she had lost. I made a conscious effort not to mention friends or even a sibling who was expecting a baby. I filtered my words and used an extra sprinkle of gentleness, for she had suffered so much. I could not even fathom her pain. Colossians 4:6 says, "Let your speech always be with grace, seasoned with salt, that you may know how you ought to answer each one." *Grace seasoned with salt?*

I stared at Julie in disbelief. We were in high school, and she had just confided in me that she was dating an unbeliever.

Thoughts bounced around in my head like a ping pong ball, and I struggled with what to say. Should I pretend to be happy for her, essentially giving my approval or tell her that what she was doing was wrong and risk our friendship? She was a Christian and unequally yoked with an unbeliever. How could I tell her that? Isn't it God's job to judge? Who am I to pass condemnation? *Let your speech always be with grace,* seasoned with salt…

Okay, Lord. I will obey. With careful words and a pounding heart, I told her that dating an unbeliever was against God's Word. Simply put, it was wrong. Silence. Crickets. I wondered if she would be angry. She said very little, and I thought my words would be ignored. However, later that year, she gave a testimony in chapel and told how she had been dating a nonbeliever, but that they were no longer together. That there was only one person who had confronted her and told her it was wrong. **One person.**

The realization of the effect of my words hit me as she sat down and leaned over to me. "That was you, you know." What would have happened if I had said the same words, without the grace? What if I had said them with judgment and condemnation? *Grace seasoned with salt.* Gently. Gently.

Christy was needy. Cried easily. Socially awkward. Not many friends. I worried that she would be clingy and want to do everything with me or call all the time. She was kind, and I enjoyed getting together with her, but I feared that I might be her only friend and didn't want that kind of responsibility. Ephesians 4:32a says, "But be ye kind to one another, tenderhearted…"

I didn't know how to handle this unique kind of friendship, but I did know that God wanted me to be compassionate and tenderhearted. I chose my words carefully during our conversations as I knew it didn't take much to bring tears to her eyes. I had seen it happen before with comments people made to her. I knew God was telling me to be gentle. She is more sensitive than others.

So I was. And the result? She wasn't clingy. She made more friends. She cried along with me when I told her of a trial God was taking me through. She didn't judge me when I told her that I had been struggling for months with tears that just wouldn't stop. Why? She was familiar with tears. She was sensitive and understood my hurt with a compassion that others couldn't understand.

It is only by God's grace that I responded with gentleness rather than judgment in these situations. I wish that I could say that is always my response, but it isn't, especially in my thoughts. Psalm 19:14 says, "Let the words of my mouth and the meditation of my heart be acceptable in your sight, Oh Lord, my Rock and my Redeemer." Not only do my words need to be acceptable in God's sight and sprinkled with kindness, but so do my thoughts.

When struggling with having the right attitude towards a particular friend or situation, my mind goes to the verse in Luke 6:31 that many of us learned as children. "Do to others as you would have them do to you." Am I responding the way I would want to be treated? Am I showing God's love both in my actions and in my heart? Not always, but I am working on it. Sanctification is a life-long process. *Kind, tenderhearted, graceful, gentle*—these are the qualities that I look for in a friend. More importantly, they are what I hope my friends see in me.

I learned some lessons the hard way when I chose not to bother reading instructions on how some garments needed to be washed and dried. Only after trying them on did I realize they shrunk and I could no longer fit them. I washed and dried the clothes with hot water and on high cotton respectively instead of washing and drying on gentle. Assumptions that "all clothes" can tolerate the same cycles can be very detrimental to one's wardrobe. Such is the case when it comes to friendships as well. We must never assume that we can all handle the same washing cycles. Some of our friends need a gentle wash. I can stretch it further by stating that each one of us does have and need a "gentle" cycle every once in a while.

Girdle Guidelines: One of my favorite lines in "R's" story is when she says, "Assumptions that 'all clothes' can tolerate the same cycle can be very detrimental to one's wardrobe. Such is the case when it comes to friendships as well." How many times have we treated all our friendships the same way? Just because Jackie can handle a harsh rebuke does not mean Susie can.

Isn't it amazing that a washing machine cycle can teach you a lesson or two about friendships? How I wish we could take this knowledge into all friendships. It takes wisdom and discernment to be able to realize which friendships need the appropriate cycle. So how then do we practice the virtue of gentleness, ladies? I believe the following will help us start the process:

- **Be willing to walk in someone's shoes before passing judgment.** I have heard countless stories of ladies who have never experienced pregnancy being cynical towards their friends who *were* pregnant and struggled with morning sickness. "It doesn't take all that," they would say, UNTIL they themselves became pregnant. It was only when they experienced the same struggle that they more understanding of the situation. We all don't need to fall pregnant to relate to someone's struggle, but a little empathy goes a long way in friendships.

- **Be slow to speak and quick to listen.** James 1:19 says, "Post this at all the intersections, dear friends: Lead with your ears, follow up with your tongue, and let anger straggle along in the rear." (MSG). Communication is all about listening. Listen! Listen! Listen! Hear the heart of the person talking to you and not how you intend to respond and fix the issue before they are done talking.

- **Take a time-out.** One of the best ways of not regretting what you said in a situation is giving yourself a time-out. If you know that your tendency is to be quick with your tongue with a dose of cynicism, give yourself a time-out. Pray and ask God to give you wisdom on how to respond. Do a roleplay of the situation with yourself to help defuse the situation with your emotions. These simple steps will help you regroup and respond in a gentler manner than you would ever imagine.

- **Practice.** 1 Corinthians 13:1-7. What a good way to self-examine when it comes to knowing how to respond gentler towards our friends when an admonition is needed. Something about that LOVE thing that works all across the board.

Let us make it our determination to become gentler friends, full of grace, but not compromising on truth. We become better for it when all is said and done.

> **The Last Word:** *"The best and simplest cosmetic for women is constant gentleness and sympathy for the noblest interests of her fellow-creatures. This preserves and gives to her features an indelibly gay, fresh, and agreeable expression. If women would but realize that harshness makes them ugly, it would prove the best means of conversion."*
>
> Berthold Auerbach

Chapter 10
Rotation Plan

"Strong women stand together when things are rough, hold each other up when they need support, and laugh together when there's no reason to."

WorkingWomen.com

Setting the Stage: Remember *Friends*, a sitcom that aired on NBC for ten seasons becoming one of the most watched and loved sitcoms of the 2000 decade? It revolved around six single friends (three men and three women) who were there for each other through thick and thin. I believe most gravitated to the show because we wanted to be part of that circle of friends. Or maybe we related to the friends that we had, and we could see those characters on TV lived out in each one of us or our friends.

Even the title of the show itself speaks volumes. It gave us permission to want to have friends and embrace their flaws and strengths through it all. The thing I liked about the show is that it focused on six friends who could "rotate" their friendships. They were not co-dependent on one person throughout the ten seasons, but Rachel found a friend in Monica when needed, but also in Phoebe, or Ross, depending on the occasion.

What about you, do you have more than one friend you can hang out with, who knows the deepest parts of you? It has been suggested that you can not have more than one close friend. But, I disagree with that notion. It is possible to have two to three meaningful, close, best friends throughout different seasons of your life (childhood friend, or college, or work/church environment). Some, of course, prefer that one friend for reasons best known to themselves and I respect that decision.

Girlfriend "T.'s" Story: I was known to be Miss Social Butterfly. I could make friends very easily and trusted every soul I met with my heart because I thought everyone I spoke with, had dinner with, worked out with, or gave me a ride to the grocery store was my "friend." I soon found out that was not the case.

Having being born and raised in a third world country, what I have shared above was the beginning of a long-lasting friendship, no questions asked. However, such was not the case when I moved to the USA. The different cultural expectations of how I viewed the formation of friendships was in stark contrast with reality. The social butterfly became "Miss Cocoon."

I had to re-adjust my expectations from one-hundred twenty miles per hour to ten miles per hour within weeks. I thought I was making long-lasting friendships, only to realize that the car ride to the grocery store was just that, a ride, or working out together was not a start to a great friendship just because we had similar interests. Even being invited to dinner was just part of a "scheme" to get to meet someone I knew so that they could use "our" friendship to connect them. But, if I did not deliver on the goods, that "friendship" was over.

It was a painful experience to walk through, but I am glad I did. Looking back, I now realize how sacred meaningful friendships are. They don't come cheap, they are earned. I slowly began setting realistic expectations on how to develop meaningful relationships. My guarded heart soon became an asset for discerning who truly wanted to be a friend with no strings attached, or someone just wanting to genuinely help because I was in need, but not to start a budding friendship.

I slowly began opening up again and became intentional in prayer for God to bring me the right kind of friends. I was in a different culture. As the proverbs say, "when in Rome, do as the Romans do," and "Rome was not built in a day." Though the process took a while, I developed four close friendships that are thriving to this day. I butt heads with each of them every so often, but I have found a home in their hearts.

Each one of them brings their own value to the table. I can share with each one different areas of my life without ever thinking I am exhausting one person with all my dysfunction. What makes it even more refreshing, is knowing that they too have other close friends they can share their personal journeys with knowing there is enough love and support to go around. It is not a competition amongst friends because we have other outlets to share life, but instead a celebration of diversity in personality and culture which makes us stronger and better human beings.

The principle is to ensure that you just don't have that one friend you pour all your problems into. You will begin to drain them, and you become like a leech-parasite. Your life becomes insatiable. You need a rotation plan because each friend handles situations differently.

Girdle Guidelines: If I went through your closet, I know I will find more than one dress, skirt, shirt, or pants. You have a variety because each of those items serves a different purpose for different occasions. Same goes for your friendships. You may not have as many friends as you do clothes, but make sure you have a few good friends you can count on at all times. Carolyn Hax, a writer with the Milwaukee Journal Sentinel states, "Open yourself to new friendships, or sit home. Or maybe more accurately, risk getting hurt or guarantee feeling lonely. I can't choose for you—but I've been hurt by old friends, too, and it's still a no-brainer to me."

So then, what does rotating friends do for you?

- **It gives you a sense of freshness in your relationships.** Your different friends give you a fresh flavor to your life. Some are spunky, some are even-keel, some are loud, some are quiet. Savor those relationships as spice to your life.

- **It broadens your worldview.** You will be able to see things from different perspectives. Imagine you are sharing with two close friends (who may not know each other) something you may be walking through. Both will advise you from two different perspectives which, in the long run, will broaden your decision-making process.

- **It grows your trust meter.** Most times we are tentative to open up to one person. Imagine how you can grow in trust with others if you give yourself an opportunity to find those safe people you can invite into your heart-space.

The Last Word: *"The person who tries to live alone will not succeed as a human being. His heart withers if it does not answer another heart. His mind shrinks away if he hears only the echoes of his own thoughts and finds no other inspiration."*

Pearl S. Buck

Chapter 11

THE RIGHT DETERGENT

"Each friend represents a world in us, a world possibly not born until they arrive, and it is only by this meeting that a new world is born."

Anaïs Nin

Setting the Stage: Without going into the details about how the chemical molecule structure of detergent works on clothes, we can all agree that the work it does is to clean clothes. Using the right kind of detergent, however, is critical to maintaining and sustaining fabric long-term. The Hour Glass Angel, a site dedicated to educating us on how to take care of shapewear states, *"It's also important to use the right type of detergent.* Specially formulated lingerie detergent works best—any detergents that contain dyes, fragrances, alcohol, softeners or bleach can irreparably damage your shapers by breaking down their construction [...] so stick to lingerie detergent only!"

As critical and important as it is to use the right type of detergent for shapewear, it is critical to have friends in our lives who will act as the right kind of detergent.

Girlfriend "S.'s" Story: All friendships have a starting pointing from which they began to grow and, just like our girdle sizes, we expand, stretching our boundaries to the point that causes them to snap without warning. I have a best friend of almost nineteen years, and in 2002 we found a toxic chemical mixture that ripped our friendship into shreds without warning.

On the same day, we both inadvertently triggered our main emotional triggers which caused us both to shut down and pull away. She triggered my greatest fear of being vulnerable, and I triggered her abandonment issues. To our amazement, we both sat stubbornly in silence; ten years quickly went without one word, and that pride cost us ten years we can never get back.

Hanging with other friends continually reminded me of how much I missed my best friend. I was too afraid to reach out and say "I'm sorry." To be honest, so much time had gone by that I wasn't even sure what had really happened. I asked God to give me a chance to say "I'm sorry" and ask for forgiveness. When the opportunity arrived, I nervously drafted my thoughts and hit the send button, feeling somewhat relieved. But, I knew that until we talked it out, I would never be sure if everything really was okay between us.

After reconnecting, she invited me to be her maid-of-honor at her wedding. Shocked, I reluctantly accepted because I felt undeserving for such an honor. Then she said, "You've always been my best friend, I asked God for one, and you're it." The strength and conviction in her voice never wavered with this belief. Today, our friendship is stronger than it ever was and our ten years apart taught us both that, no matter what, we *must* communicate—even when we don't feel like it.

Back then we thought that we really knew each other, but now I can truly say that I trust her with my life. She is no longer my best friend, but she is my sister. Humility, grace and forgiveness, the right detergent, in this case, are what reconnected us and what is holding us together today. We don't take it for granted that we're sister-friends. We listen to each other, speak our honest opinions, and stand beside each other when no words can be spoken. We both grew up with totally opposite backgrounds—me in foster care and her with a huge, close-knit, loving family. Our differences help balance out our friendship.

Girdle Guidelines: Realizing that specific garments require specific detergents got me thinking about why that was the case. I discovered that detergents are made of different surfactants—surface-active agents; these agents have to be used to address the specific need of the garments, removing oils, soils, grease, etc. According to Home and Garden, "The prime benefit of surfactants is their ability to draw grime out of clothing while making sure it doesn't return to the fabrics."

I believe that each one of us has "surface-active agents" when it comes to our relationships. These agents are to be used to better relationships and not destroy them. We all get soiled, greasy, and release funky smells with our lives. Things like being cynical, negative, judgmental, bitter, etc. (knowing or unknowingly) taint our lives. This is why it's critical to have girdle girlfriends who can come alongside you and act like surfactants—helping remove that grime before it affects the fabric of your life, which is your HEART!

Below are some of the surfactants that you need to be in your girlfriend's life, or vice versa, to help them be that fresh garment each day they walk the face of the earth:

- **Be Discerning**: Know which agent to use when your friend needs it in order for it to work in their lives. Sometimes you may know the "what," but not the "when." Timing is everything. Trust God to lead you in this area as you pray for direction.

- **Use the Right Words**: Proverbs 25:11 states, "Like apples of gold in settings of silver is a word spoken in right circumstances." Please use your words wisely and carefully. They should include one hundred percent of grace, truth, and love. Let that word that you speak wash the soiled areas of your friend's life. Your goal is to "brighten and whiten" the garments of someone's heart.

- **Be Patient**: Most changes don't happen overnight, so please have patience with your friends who are walking through life's hard journey until they are able to overcome. Pull back and try to walk in their shoes and determine if that is how you would like to be treated if the tables were turned.

In her book, "I Quit!," Geri Scazzero says, "Choosing an authentic life does not mean choosing an easy life; these decisions are difficult and involve pain. The question is whether the pain you choose will be redemptive or destructive." When you decide to be the right surfactant, you are declaring that you want an authentic life, one that wants to build and not tear down; one that wants to speak truth and not lies; one that wants the best for your friends and not the worst. When you choose this approach, you may be rejected by those who don't subscribe to your values. It will be painful for a while, but you will be thankful you chose redemption over destruction.

> **The Last Word:** *"A foolish man may be known for six things; anger without cause, speech without profit, change without progress, inquiry without object, putting trust in a stranger, and mistaking foes for friends."*
>
> Arabic Proverb

Chapter 12
What Kind of Girdle Are You?

"In the long run, we shape our lives, and we shape ourselves. The process never ends until we die. And the choices we make are ultimately our own responsibility."

Eleanor Roosevelt

One of my favorite books that has had an impact on my paradigm on friendships to date is "The People Factor," by Van Moody. Some of the areas that he covers in the book are critical laws of relationships, the first being, "You've Got to Be You-The Law of Being Real."

He states,

"If you are going to be real, you must demand honesty from yourself and avoid self-deception. The easiest person in

FINAL THOUGHT

the world to deceive is yourself. Think about it: You can so easily tell yourself you are smarter, more attractive, more creative, more loyal, more honest, or more *anything* than you actually are. And whatever you tell yourself, you believe. Believing your own personal campaign is easy, but it will not lead to truth, transparency, and integrity. One of the best ways to really get to know yourself is to focus on your behavior rather than your words [...] The better you know yourself, the better your relationships will be."

I am pretty sure we have all encountered that one girlfriend who blames everyone else but herself for her failed relationships. She never takes responsibility for her actions. She can never keep long-lasting friendships. I sometimes wonder if she truly believes that she has no role to play in the outcome of her relationships or if she is just pretending.

You are also familiar with this response: when the preacher is preaching a sermon that you strongly believe is meant for your friend and you never seem to ask yourself that one important question, could this message be for me?

The key to any successful relationship is knowing your own heart, your emotions, your will, and your mind. Without taking responsibility for how you respond and accept correction will surely make for a miserable outcome in life with friendships. However, asking yourself those tough questions without placing the blame on others (like, "Why can't I sustain long-term relationships?" "Why do I get easily offended?" "Why do I always see myself as a victim?" etc. etc.) will help you begin the process of being a healthy soul—mentally, emotionally, and socially.

Be that friend that you want others to be to you. If you want loyalty, be loyal. If you want grace extended, extend grace! If you want others to trust you, stop the gossip! Determine to be healthy for your sake and the sake of others.

Making friends is not an easy task. Sometimes, because of what one has been through with hurtful friendships, we tend to want to self-protect. Dr. Larry Crabb, a psychologist, shares some meaningful insight about this need to self-protect. He calls it the "sin of self-protection." He states, "The sin of self-protection [...] occurs when our legitimate thirst for receiving love creates a demand not to be hurt that overrides a commitment to lovingly involve ourselves with others."

He goes on to say that "when that demand for self-protection interferes with our willingness to move towards others with their well-being in view, then the law of love is violated." We will hurt each other on this journey called life. We will be disappointed, and we will disappoint, but let us not use these excuses to not find, develop and sustain meaningful relationships. The world needs you desperately!

The Very Last Words

"But until a person can say deeply and honestly, 'I am what I am today because of the choices I made yesterday,' that person cannot say, 'I choose otherwise.'"

– **Stephen R. Covey**

FINAL THOUGHT

"What we call our destiny is truly our character and that character can be altered. The knowledge that we are responsible for our actions and attitudes does not need to be discouraging, because it also means that we are free to change this destiny."

– **Anaïs Nin**

"You are essentially who you create yourself to be and all that occurs in your life is the result of your own making."

– **Stephen Richards**

"But what happens when we live God's way? He brings gifts into our lives, much the same way that fruit appears in an orchard—things like affection for others, exuberance about life, serenity. We develop a willingness to stick with things, a sense of compassion in the heart, and a conviction that a basic holiness permeates things and people. We find ourselves involved in loyal commitments, not needing to force our way in life, able to marshal and direct our energies wisely."

– **Galatians 5:22 MSG**

Notes

The Sisterhood of Girdles and Girlfriends

1. Mayo Clinic, Available from https://en.wikipedia.org/wiki/Mayo_Clinic; Internet; accessed January 3, 2016.
2. Mayo Clinic Staff, *Enrich Your Life and Improve Your Health*, Available from http://www.mayoclinic.org/healthy-lifestyle/adult-health/in-depth/friendships/art-20044860/; Internet; accessed January 10, 2016.
3. Nell Lake, CommonHealth, *Midnight Friends: How Wired Patients are Transforming Chronic Illness*, Available from http://commonhealth.wbur.org/2014/05/midnight-friends-wired-patients-chronic-illness; Internet; accessed on April 19, 2016.
4. Leslie Parrott, *Soul Friends: What Every Woman Needs to Grow in Her Faith*. (Grand Rapids, MI: Zondervan), 2015
5. Kingsley Felix, *The Emotional and Physical Health of Wearing a Girdle*, Available from http://www.healthable.org/health-benefits-wearing-girdle/; internet; accessed January 12, 2016.
6. Andy Stanley, *Enemies of the Heart: Breaking Free from*

Four Emotions That Control You." (Colorado Springs: Multnomah Books, 2011).

How to Shop for Girdles and Girlfriends

1. Ehow.Org, *How to Buy Girdles*, Available from http://www.ehow.com/how_2189545_buy-girdles.html; Internet; accessed February 9, 2016.

2. Mayo Clinic, *What are Some Ways to Meet People*, Available from http://www.mayoclinic.org/healthy-lifestyle/adult-health/in-depth/friendships/art-20044860?pg=2; Internet; accessed April 20, 2016.

3. Matthew Kelly, Rhythms of Life: Living Everyday with Passion and Purpose. Revised ed. (Beacon Publishing: 2004)

The Right Style

1. Brené Brown, *The Gift of Imperfection: Letting Go of Who you Think You're Supposed to Be and Embrace Who You Are.* MN: Hazelden, 2010)

Try It on First

1. Ebay, *The Dos and Don'ts of Wearing Shapewear,"* Available from http://www.ebay.co.uk/gds/The-Dos-and-Donts-of-Wearing-Shapewear-/10000000177630036/g.html; Internet; accessed April 25, 2016.

2. Tim A. Gardner, *The Naked Soul: God's Amazing Everyday Solution to Loneliness.* (Colorado Springs: Waterbrook, 2004).

Fit Matters

1. Tim A. Gardner, *The Naked Soul: God's Amazing Everyday Solution to Loneliness.* (Colorado Springs: Waterbrook, 2004).

Improves Your Posture

1. Health: *10 Ways to have Great Posture as you Age*, Available from http://www.health.com/health/gallery/0,,20446224,00.html; internet; Accessed April 14, 2016.
2. Posturebly: *5 Negative Effects of your body and your mind*, Available from http://posturebly.com/5-negative-effects-of-bad-posture-on-your-body-and-mind; internet; Accessed April 14, 2016.
3. Healthable: *The Emotional and Physical Benefits of Wearing a Girdle*, Available from http://www.healthable.org/health-benefits-wearing-girdle/; internet; Accessed April 14, 2016.
4. Gary Smalley, *The DNA of Relationships: Discover How you are Designed for Satisfying Relationships* (Ill: Tyndale House, 2004).

The Muffin Top Concealer

1. Jennifer Walters, *Shape: The Pros and Cons of Spanx and Other Shapewear*, Available from, http://www.shape.com/latest-news-trends/pros-and-cons-spanx-and-other-shapewear; Internet; accessed April 29, 2016.

Wash on Gentle

1. Merriam-Webster Dictionary, Available from http://www.merriam-webster.com/dictionary/gentleness; internet; accessed April 13, 2016.
2. Virtue First Foundation: *Promoting Virtue to Rebuild the Character of America's Youth*, Available from http://virtuefirst.org/virtues/gentleness/;internet; accessed April 13, 2016.

Rotation Plan

1. Carolyn Hax, *Friendship Has Risks and Rewards*, Available from www.jsonline.com; internet; accessed April 6, 2016.

The Right Detergent

1. Hourglass Angel, *Essential Tips for Shapewear Care: Shapewear Guidelines*, Available from http://www.hourglassangel.com/blog/essential-tips-shapewear-care/; Internet; accessed April 5, 2016.
2. Emily Frydendall, *How Laundry Detergent Works: Surfactants: Laundry Detergent Cleaning Power*, Available from http://home.howstuffworks.com/laundry-

detergent1.htm; Internet; accessed April 6, 2016.
3. Geri Scazerro with Peter Scazerro, "I Quit: Stop Pretending Everything is Fine and Change Your Life." (Grand Rapids: Zondervan, 2010)

What Kind of Girdle Are You?

1. Vanable Moody, *The People Factor: How Building Great Relationships and Ending Bad Ones Unlocks Your God-Given Purpose* (Nashville: TN. Nelson Books, 2014)
2. Larry Crabb, *Inside Out: Real Change is Possible if you're willing to start from the inside.* Expanded 10th Anniversary ed. (Navpress, 1998).
3. Ibid.

www.ingramcontent.com/pod-product-compliance
Lightning Source LLC
Chambersburg PA
CBHW021445080526
44588CB00009B/700